DATE DUE

PRINTED IN U.S.A.

PUSHES AND PULLS

By
Steffi Cavell-Clarke

Published in 2017 by
KidHaven Publishing, an Imprint of Greenhaven Publishing, LLC
353 3rd Avenue
Suite 255
New York, NY 10010

Designer: Danielle Jones
Editor: Grace Jones

Cataloging-in-Publication Data

Names: Cavell-Clarke, Steffi.
Title: Pushes and pulls / Steffi Cavell-Clarke.
Description: New York : KidHaven Publishing, 2017. | Series: First science | Includes index.
Identifiers: ISBN 9781534520806 (pbk.) | ISBN 9781534520820 (library bound) | ISBN 9781534520813 (6 pack) | ISBN 9781534520837 (ebook)
Subjects: LCSH: Force and energy–Juvenile literature.
Classification: LCC QC73.4 C38 2017 | DDC 531'.6–dc23

Printed in the United States of America

CPSIA compliance information: Batch #CW17KL: For further information contact Greenhaven Publishing LLC, New York, New York at 1-844-317-7404.

Please visit our website, www.greenhavenpublishing.com. For a free color catalog of all our high-quality books, call toll free 1-844-317-7404 or fax 1-844-317-7405.

PHOTO CREDITS

Abbreviations: l-left, r-right, b-bottom,
t-top, c-center, m-middle.

Front cover – Pressmaster. 2 – Sergey Novikov. 4 – sunabesyou.
5 – Sergey Novikov. 6 – Valua Vitaly. 7 – Duplass. 8 – Jorge Casais. 9 –Veronica Louro.
10 – sainthorantdaniel. 11 – Jim Lopes. 12 – Hatchapong Palurtchaivong. 13 – colors.
14 – Julia Kuznetsova. 15 – Pressmaster. 16 – DnDavis. 17 – Halfpoint. 18 – Sergei Kolesnikov.
19 –TairA. 20 – MarcusVDT. 21 – janecocoa. 22l&r – Lucie Lang. 22m – My_inspiration.
23tl – Narintorn_m2. 23bl – John99. 23tr – Ledimup. 23br – oksana2-10.
Images are courtesy of Shutterstock.com.
With thanks to Getty Images, Thinkstock Photo, and iStockphoto.

CONTENTS

Words that look like this can be found in the glossary on page 24.

What Is SCIENCE?

What does a force do?

What is the difference between a push and a pull?

What makes things move?

Science can answer many difficult questions we may have and help us understand the world around us.

What Is a FORCE?

A force makes something move. You cannot see a force, but you can see and feel its **effects**.

This is a push.

This is a pull.

Pushes and pulls are two different types of forces.

How Do You PUSH and PULL?

push

You can push shopping carts in a supermarket.

You use your body to push things away from you.
You usually push things to make them move forward.

You can also use your body
to pull **objects** toward you.

Each team is
pulling the
rope toward
them.

pull

pull

Natural
FORCES

There are **natural** forces that can push and pull, too. Wind is a natural force.

Wind is moving air. You can see its effect as it pushes through the trees.

Changing
SHAPE

Push and pull forces can change the shape of things by squashing, stretching, or bending them.

You can push or pull soft clay
to make many different shapes.

Changing
DIRECTION

Pushes and pulls can change the **direction**
of a moving object.

Soccer players use their feet to push a soccer ball. They can push the ball in different directions.

Changing SPEED

Pushes and pulls can make an object move faster or slower. The harder an object is pushed, the faster and farther it will travel.

Pulling can slow down an object that is moving in the opposite direction.

STOPPING

Pushing or pulling against a moving object can make it stop.

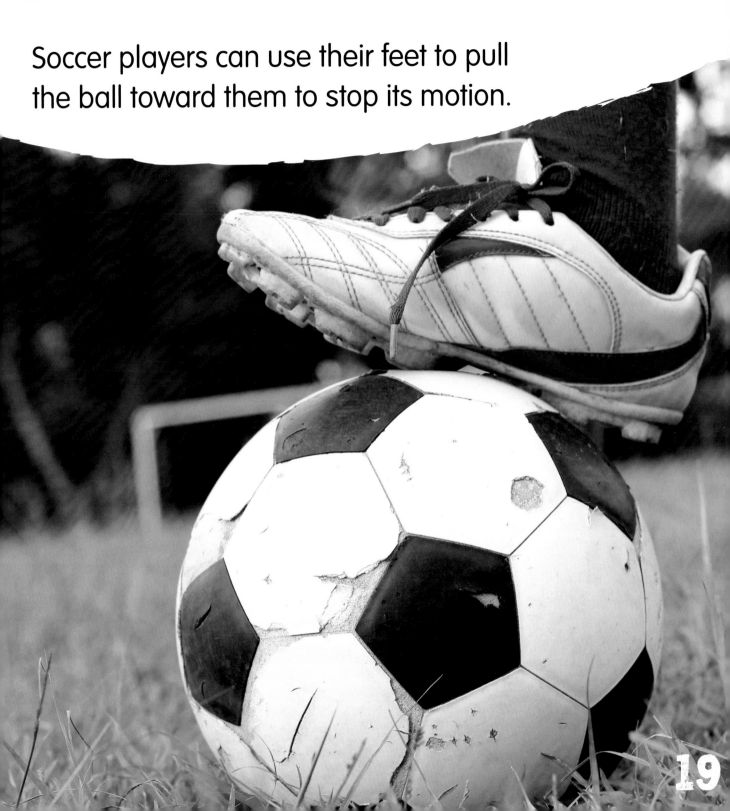

Soccer players can use their feet to pull the ball toward them to stop its motion.

19

GRAVITY

Gravity is a force that pulls everything down toward the ground.

You are able to see the effects of gravity when you let go of an object, because it falls to the ground.

21

Let's EXPERIMENT!

How can we use a force to change the shape of an object? Let's find out!

YOU WILL NEED:

blue clay
red clay
yellow clay
a clean surface

STEP 1

Place the blue clay on a clean surface.
Use your hands to push the clay, and then roll it between your hand and the surface.

STEP 2

Pick up the red clay. Use your hands to push and roll the clay into a round ball.

TOP TIP:
Ask an adult to help you!

STEP 3

Now, pick up the yellow clay, and pull it apart to make smaller pieces.

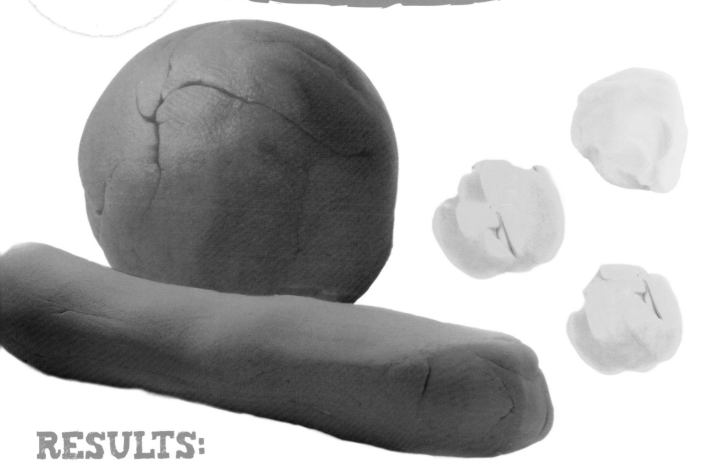

RESULTS:

Look at the different shapes you have made. This shows you how pushes and pulls can change the shape of objects.

23

GLOSSARY

clay   a natural material used to make things
direction   the way something is moving
effects   the results of something
natural   something existing in nature, not made
             by people or machines
objects   things that can been seen and touched

INDEX